ALSO BY CLAUDIA GARY

Ripples in the Fabric
Schadenfreud(e)
Humor Me
Bikini Buyer's Remorse
Let's Get Out of Here
The Grateful Guest
Epicurigrams
Genetic Revisionism
Someone Likes You

photo by Matthew Lennig

The Author at 15

TIME AND OTHER SOLVENTS

ISBN: 979-8-99925-687-4

Library of Congress Copyright Registration Pending
(Application Case Number 1-15083547951)

Cover image and book design by Alan Abrams

Sligo Creek Publishing
9039 Sligo Creek Parkway
Silver Spring, MD 20901
sligocreekpublishing.com

TIME AND OTHER SOLVENTS

a story of healing, told in poems

by CLAUDIA GARY

*For my beloved kids,
kids-in-law, and grandkids,
who honor the arts with their talents
and who make me happy.*

CONTENTS

The author and her parents

PROLOGUE

AMERICAN DREAMERS

From Sputnik to Apollo,
scrambling, climbing, falling,
the dream we chased was hollow.
Somehow the muse kept calling
and I could only follow.

Determined in the '50s to give all
in search of the American Dream, he dropped
his family name to avoid prejudice.
She dropped whatever brain cells made her cry,
thanks to electroconvulsive therapy.

Determined in the '60s to succeed,
they left New York with dishes, couch, *New Yorker,*
to move five times, making and leaving friends
till gold was theirs at last—but it was hollow.
And then they lost it all and lost each other.

Determined to make sense of it, their firstborn
scribbled in notebooks she called "Mobile Home"
through the mid-'70s, then doubled down
on sugar-numbed, sated oblivion,
until she clambered back to poetry.

Through Sputnik and Apollo,
scrambling, climbing, falling,
the dream we won was hollow,
but still the muse keeps calling.
How can I fail to follow?

PART I

WHAT CAN GO WRONG?

ATLANTIC BEACH

Paint blisters carry cabanas.
Cabanas deliver Atlantic Beach
onto memory's beach—not stepwise
but in waves through sunken castles.

Memory, love, composed alike,
are just at arm's length this evening.

When we would arrive at Atlantic Beach
the air rippled over hot tarmac.
Out on the sand were grain-filled towels,
shovels and pails and sifters.

We rode the waves with mothers and aunts,
goggled, skirted, slathered.

Cabanas smelled of suntan oil,
not sunblock cream—yet here we are.
Blisters that burst at fingertips
were lead-based paint—yet here we are.

Wind from a beach umbrella
escapes to my inland roof tonight

and memory/love, mocking the tide,
whistles and whispers in one warm breath
through naked-pink shells
composing our selves.

BEACH MOSAIC

After they cracked beneath
my feet in wet brown-sugar sand,
I dropped them in the color pail:

white as my fresh new teeth,
tan as my summer face and hand,
smooth as a new-filed fingernail,

blue as my eyes or brown as our hair.
These were for Mommy's mosaic.
I know now she thought hard

but also lightly about where
to place them so she'd make
the shape of every shard

cling to a lovely pattern not
too simple, or complex,
or obvious, but still

detectable. And what she taught
without a word or text
merged with the ocean's thrill.

SHADING

Before making a mark, I broke three rules:
snapping apart a darkly colored crayon;
peeling one half completely (zero cover,
abundant color); then turning it sideways
to drag and swirl its width across the paper.
Here was my shadow, yours, the universe
without a star. Standing the crayon up,
I drew stick figures. They, too, would need shadows.

FINGERPAINT

This kind of paint was only used in school,
since we already knew too much: mosaics,
gold leaf, tracing, creating plaster casts
of hands and feet when we went to the beach.
Connect-the-dots, coloring, sewing cards,
and fingerpaint? Those were just busywork.
Mother knew art, and I knew it was magic.

CHILDHOOD, REVISED

I never cut my fingertip
on a stray blade, nor did I slip

while chasing the Good Humor truck
and bump my head on it. Good luck

forever held me in its graces.
Playgrounds, too, were friendly places.

Mom went away for just two weeks
to rest and study art techniques.

Flowers bloomed on the balcony
when she returned. Her memory

remained intact. She held me near
for decades to abolish fear.

GUIDANCE

What can go wrong if Mama, a fine artist,
cuddles me in her lap, places a crayon
in my right hand, then takes my hand in hers
and draws a line with me? The crayon breaks,

but I can choose another. Paper tears,
but she can turn the page. The table wobbles,
but there's cardboard to place under its leg.
The dog is howling at a fire engine—

another mimic in the house. And next
some watercolor. This is fun. The dish
of water spills. She mops it up. I take
the brush in my hand now, all by myself,

and my brushstroke resembles hers. A gift,
an artist for a mother. Mama wonders
how long this joy can last before she breaks.
When she was a young girl, her mother sometimes

would slap her face in front of all her cousins.
But now she takes my hand, guides it across
the paper. What can go wrong?

HANDEDNESS

She had the best intentions
for teaching me to favor
the right hand.

Conformity was one,
orderly script another,
and no trail

of smudged ink in the wake
of leftward-tilted letters
as with Dad

whose parents let him be
till teachers tried their best
but soon failed.

So Mom knew to start early.
It helped that I was quick,
mastering

even her drawing style
taught by her hand on mine:
puppetry

rendered complete at last
when I forgot which hand
was in charge.

THE WOMAN WHO JUMPED

You remember more
than I. They only told me
after years had fallen
across the memory.

You and I were neighbors,
small, in love with life.
Then one night she fell
down past a balcony—

maybe yours. I heard
sirens in the street,
gossips in the hall,
words I didn't yet know.

Men came stomping up
and down the fire escape.
Flashlights danced around—
maybe in my window.

What about the angel,
the dazzling beam of light,
the resonating voice?
"Don't be afraid," it said.

Isn't that what angels say?
Or was it a policeman
or fireman consoling
while checking on the dead?

MORNING, 1956

Beside our sunken living room, my parents
sat at the kitchen table and refilled
their swirled-gray coffee cups, discussing merits
of Eisenhower versus Stevenson,
Kefauver versus Nixon. Static-ridden,

each candidate debate on radio
would chip away the smooth consistency
of our routine. I heard an edge in each
parental voice, until I said, "Why don't you
both stay home on Election Day?" But soon

my mother introduced me to the metal
machines with turning levers, crisp white labels
printed authoritatively with black
letters. She probably helped elect Ike.
The next day, breakfast time was back to normal:

She would stir half-and-half into her coffee
and Dad would show her why there was no need
to stir it, as the pouring made it blend
and settle, more or less, into a bitter
sweetness that they would sometimes let me taste.

PERFECT TIME

I. Subway Ride, 1956

The turnstile clinked over our brazen fare,
then opened to a world of pitch black, hollow
and without ends. Its name was everywhere,
spelled in mosaic, voiced for us to follow:
"Van Wyck Boulevard!" where a train called F
would sweep us to the zoo or the museum.
Who cared if tunnel noise might make us deaf
and leather straps held germs? We couldn't see them.
The nickel chocolate bars, gum for a penny,
dropped through their own turnstiles and rode along.
We nibbled them until there weren't any,
but you and I were happy with a song
in echoed harmony, rhythm and rhyme,
sweet Mother that you were in perfect time.

II. Clinic, 1957

Perfect time's up. A brittle stick of chalk,
you're quivering, sobbing, packing for somewhere.
"Just for a while," says Daddy. "You can talk
by telephone, and visit. She needs care."

You show me pansies in the clinic garden.
"They all have little velvet faces....See?"
From one trip to the next you seem to harden.
I didn't know about the E.C.T.[1]

Back home at last, you have a new perfection,
a measured beauty, fretting at your age.
You welcome only half of my affection,
give me a marble angel. In a rage
I break it. You repair it. You are strong
but now no longer happy in our song.

---

[1] electroconvulsive therapy

DOLLHOUSE

On loan from my older cousin
it had shiny painted walls.

I was four the day my mother
came home from the hospital
after several long months

and several electroshock treatments.
I ran and clung to her

but after half a minute
she called me *sticky chewing gum*
and told me to let go.

I ran back to my room.
Now grown, I have no memory

of what I might have done there.
My cousin says that when
the dollhouse was returned

there were black crayon scribbles
on every upstairs wall.

GETTING LOST

In childhood dreams I once got double-crossed.
Familiar homes and sidewalks grown confusing,
I found myself afraid of getting lost.

My dream of wandering farther from the mossed
rock-garden soil where grandmother was choosing
flowers to plant—that dream got double-crossed.

Each townhouse on the block had been embossed
with the same brickwork pattern. Losing, losing,
finding myself afraid of getting lost,

of bad men in disguise who might accost
and lead me to the wrong house, disabusing
me of my faith in dreams—double-crossed

into a different life—I turned and tossed,
beat on my chest, awoke, but found no bruising,
no traces of the fear that I had lost.

Patterns of bricks, words, music, inexhaust-
ible in variation, began oozing
out of that childhood dream once double-crossed.
I found myself through fear of getting lost.

ANTISEPTIC

My father dabbed peroxide on my foot
and watched it bubble where there'd been a splinter,
reminding him of something he had learned
from training in the Air Force. "It's surprising,"
he said, "but you will never be without
an antiseptic, if you use your urine."

My mother shouted from the next room, "Hey!
Don't tell her things like that!" I sensed a strange
new light, but couldn't say just what it was
or whether it was pretty. Pretty meant
so much to Mother: pretty furniture,
sculpture and bric-a-brac beside the window

to cast unusual shadows. Pretty, too,
were glimmers of the 59th Street Bridge
as seen from Sutton Place in bumpy-textured
new paintings by a cranky relative.
But what was wedged below the prettiness,
and how far down? Was it buried too deep

to tweeze it out and cleanse the wound? I soon
would find an elixir captured between
décor and rough landscape, between alluring
reflections of an old bridge on the oil-
slicked surface of a long-polluted river
and fish you mustn't eat, swimming below.

AUNT ROSE

Young ladies in their rubber bathing caps
swim measured strokes across the basement pool
of the Barbizon Hotel. Not an ear, not a curl
is visible. Their strong-legged kicks resound

as Aunt Rose shows me geometric wall tiles
and ropes of floaters bobbling between lanes.
We stroll next door where blue-clad Peter Rabbit
looks up at me from glossy-coated paper

pressed, bound, and cut. His mouse friends sort bright beads.
A kitten nearly gets baked in a dumpling.
With this month's new book in a crinkly package,
Aunt Rose takes my small hand and walks me back

to her own lobby shop, joining my mother
amid the shelves of thin-boxed shiny nylons.
The dried-off swimmers march in on high heels,
then out again. How straight their stocking seams!

Rose isn't my real aunt but one whose nephew
died in the Navy during World War II,
leaving a girl who would have been his bride.
The young girl pulled together, studied art,

got a job, went to a dance, and found a husband.
They had two baby girls whose ties to Rose
are echoed splashes, chlorine-rubber air,
mosaic tiles, beige silk, synthetic mesh,

and stubby books whose sweet aroma floats
through and around me as I fan the pages.

DISCOVERING CLASSICAL MUSIC
Ludwig van Beethoven, *Symphony No. 5*

Beside the toy piano,
a kiddie phonograph
has a carousel-shaped mirror
that spins and makes me laugh—

Praxinoscope, whose pictures
accompany each song.
Wondering how the music twirls
ducklings and frogs along,

I learn to load and operate
the magical device
all by myself, then graduate
to thinner discs with more than twice
        the playtime, half the speed.

Soon Beethoven confronts me:
four strident notes, one urgent truth,
a thunderbolt that haunts me,
sustaining, then dissolving youth.
        And this is all I need.

UNDER THE PIANO

Some days it was a playhouse
with stubby shelves for me
while she played Debussy.

I sheltered like a stray mouse
in comfort and in tune,
absorbing Clair de Lune.

The damper pedal's hiccup
allowed a little wave
of sound to misbehave.

Sitting on knees, I'd pick up
my canisters of beads
to find what a mouse needs

for serving cakes to Mozart
and watching Mommy's feet.
The afternoon complete,

I could feel every note start.
Reverberating tones
massaged my growing bones.

From time to time I'd speak up
from under everything
and claim my turn to sing.

A miniature teacup
vibrated on the wood
where each crescendo stood.

GRACE
"A Dancer's World" (film), Martha Graham, 1957

As a child I saw Graham
on film, her sinewed body
flowing across the stage.

Instantly I knew
hers was the only way
I wanted to grow old.

While applying makeup
she said a dancer's world
was the heart of man

(although most of the dancers
in the film were women),
and that two precious things,

spontaneity
and simplicity,
required years of work.

Here the camera showed
a mirrored studio,
arms and legs flexing, stretching,

partners bending toward
and away from each other,
poised in repose and motion.

"You have so little time
to be reborn to the instant,"
she said before she turned

abruptly exiting
into her next performance.

AN AWAKENING

I find her name scrawled lightly under "Maid"
in Mom's phone book from when we lived in Dallas
mid-century. Ever since then she's stayed
safe in the basement of my memory palace,
where warm southern air yields to the perfume
of ironing fresh linen tablecloths,
silk shirts and handkerchiefs, making them bloom
unscorched, protecting them from hungry moths.

She showed me how to smooth a cotton collar
with the hot iron's point, asking what I'd
studied that day, claiming I was a scholar,
since all except First Grade she'd been denied.
I frowned, confused, and asked how that could be.
Gracious despite such wrongs, she smiled at me.

HOME MOVIE, CIRCA 1960

I stop the film just after the bears, as promised.
Enough. You've seen how each one stood on hind legs,
sweating into its fur in the Yellowstone sun,
pressing its paws and belly against the car door,

eating graham crackers, its back to the movie camera
my father held. He watched for any sign
of discontent lest the bear turn around
and notice him. But no, the routine worked:

Dad always managed to dash around the car,
climb back behind the wheel, slam the door shut,
and get us away. You couldn't see that on film
nor could you see me, six-year-old accomplice

in the back seat with a box of honey grahams
held tight on my lap, breaking up the crackers
along their dotted lines, counting out groups
of four for Mom to slip out to the bear

through her all-but-closed window. Sure, you saw
the telescopic moose, the faces of cliffs
in a too-slow panorama of the park,
the stillness I would only grant for movies,

the wiles my mother lavished on the lens
when Dad recalled he was no camera—but not
the paw prints, sweat marks, kept on the car for weeks,
trophies of two kids who passed for parents.

FIRST VALENTINE

"To my darling, I love you, from Mommy"

She tried to teach me all she knew
of art. She was my queen.
I watched as she imagined new
arrangements for this scene.
I saw her dab the milky glue
to make all edges clean.

Red velvet heart on paper, gold
corners and frames embossed,
die-cut, elegantly controlled,
assert that nothing's lost
in Mommy's domain. Did she hold
a mirror to the cost

of making all seem beautiful?
She needed it, of course,
because her love was volatile
and distanced from its source.
Besides, all things were possible
if one could apply force.

Four cheerful angels gather,
each robed in pink or blue,
around her cursive blather.
Or could the words be true?
Of course that's what I'd rather
believe—and I'm there too,

stuck in a tiny oval frame
on which a butterfly
leans in to greet me, says my name,
assures me she will try
to make her love real, stanch my blame.
She asks me not to cry.

Detailing a Picture Frame

Making it clear that nothing has escaped
her scrutiny, she coats a brush with pink,
then gold, to fill each gap where time has scraped
away the textured trim. She paints a link
from loss to pleasure, penury to riches,
her muted tones a silent commentary.
With surface matte and gold edge she bewitches
this frame beyond the portrait it will carry
to generations who may only know her
through her exacting touch, both cruel and tender.
Only a hint of the imagined roar—
the artists' voices and the ancient splendor
she studied in her own youth—will they trace
in wood surrounding her young daughter's face.

PART II

IF I HAD WINGS

HIDE AND SEEK

Pavel Tchelitchew, *"Cache-Cache" (Hide and Seek)*,
1940-42, Museum of Modern Art, New York:
https://www.moma.org/collection/works/79501?locale=en

Young girl with butterfly before a tree,
or entering the tree, or the broad hand-
shaped shadow it unfolds: You could be me.
Half-hidden faces watch and understand,
their features frozen and their pulses brisk,
how they and you and I must be connected.
The tree becomes a cave where you will risk
losing yourself to find what you expected.

Then why pursue it anyway? *you ask*
these children, infants, who surround the womb
concealing, nourishing you for the task
of self-discovery. It's here you'll bloom.

Without forgetting hurt, you may forgive
and reexamine life. Then you can live.

MOZART'S ALPHABET

I.

Whenever Mrs. Glicker babysits,
she brings crochet hooks and a ball of twine.
While Mom and Dad see movies, she outwits
toy stores and factories: She can design
a sweater for each doll in your collection—
sometimes a dress or skirt—and turn it out,
a swirly-patterned wool or lace confection,
all in an evening's work. You have no doubt
she is the best, so when she asks one day,
"Are you folks Jewish?" you, of course, will need
to ask your mother. Mom says, in dismay,
"I've been remiss!" and soon you have a creed.
Mom's insecurity has lit a fire.
At least the cantor lets you join the choir.

II.

Each week you have to learn a Hebrew text
and taste the flavors of a holiday—
Hamen's hat stuffed with poppy seeds is next—
but since this is *your* story, we can say
the sweetest thing you find that year at Temple
is polyphonic music you can sing.
Soprano, Alto, Tenor, Bass, are ample
with no part sung by any god or king.

A choral alphabet may have been meant
as practice, but for you it reigns supreme:
unlike the school tune, this is eloquent.
This alphabet spells heaven in your dream.

Some other song may hold words of a prayer,
but those are just words. This song takes you there.

ON READING THE ENCYCLOPEDIA

When Dad suggested this, at first you stalled.
Was *that* why he had bought it? Oh, you knew
some kids who claimed to read each volume through,
page after page—show-offs, as they were called—
all boys. Some boys were okay. Most appalled.
Those who inspired you were very few.
Dad was a rarity. What could you do
but take the bait? You started out enthralled,
but soon your curiosity declined
till you devised a game of deftly chasing
cross-references. *See also,* said each one,
and you'd be off to flex your agile mind
on worlds criss-crossing, insights interlacing.
How lucky that your father had no son.

MOUNTAIN FIRE

*"Sunday, November the 5th, 1961, was hot and windy in
Los Angeles.... As dawn approached on Monday the
6th... Fire Station 92 [received] a teletype from
headquarters, noting the day would be considered a
'high hazard' day in the Santa Monica mountains..."*
—Los Angeles Fire Department Historical Society

Who is this with a garden hose
on a gravel roof, watering wind,
ignoring pleas from firemen?
Oh yes, he knows,

but can't stop. Neighbors' houses broil
to concrete slabs with chimneys,
melted-down pipes, dead brush and trees,
eroded soil.

Wild Santa Ana wind has tossed
burning wood shingles, leveling
castles, condos. Leave everything
or you'll be lost.

Later in the newsreel,
a mother steers her family's car
down Roscomare, and there we are,
too scared to feel.

An offer on the radio
says "Stay for free at Disneyland!"
Mother and daughter drive and plan,
deciding No.

Allowed back, they are lucky: See?
Fire has spared their modest home.
The child's toy bin contains a poem.
Unscathed—or isn't she?

ANNOUNCEMENT

Mom takes you on a lunch date, someplace chic
in early 1962 L.A.
She's been mysterious but now can speak.
"You'll be a sister soon!" you hear her say
with her slow, careful smile, indelible
pink lipstick outlined with a little brush,
then colored in. Her dress is oddly full
but no less elegant. Did she just blush?

Eight-and-a-half, you shrug your shoulders, since
this *can't* be as unnerving as the flames
that grazed your house last fall. With chewy mints
you ladies leave for home, discussing names.

Back in your room you hug yourself with glee.
At long last, maybe soon she'll let you be.

Somewhere in the San Fernando Valley

An adobe village you built at age eight
with six huts each the size of your palm
along a path to a mission modeled
on San Juan Capistrano
is now buried under a swimming pool
the next owner installed.

Pachysandra ground cover
and purple-flowered succulents
your mother carefully arranged
between the street and picture window
must have stopped wandering
when new additions walled them in.

Still visible on Google Earth
is the driveway where you and your father
launched again and again a shiny
cardboard rocket whose NASA-decaled
nose cone was easier to find
if you aimed straight for heaven.

You never found the tiny brass
mission bell but still can hear
its angelic sound.

HOME ECONOMICS

Measuring, sewing, cooking
combined to build a language
material and warm
within this room of girls.

You were attentive, made it
your business to discover
how to run a household
despite your mother's life.

Although founded on science,
food preservation's safety
became a hiding place
when her family descended.

There in the yellow kitchen
among glass bowls and covers
you heard familiar edges
of pride, ambition, envy,

domestic expectations,
dramas and disappointments
through the white glossy swinging
door where your father once

had caught his hand and stopped
dead still as he realized
removing it would hurt
regardless of direction.

THE DINING ROOM WAR, 1967

At dinnertime the first volleys are fired
above your fork, knife, spoon, chocolate-smeared plate.
Soon you're too sugar-high to concentrate
on homework and can hardly sleep, tripwired
to the war on TV. Although you're tired
next day in history class, it's far too late
for an exemption: conscientious hate
soars through your veins. You are already mired
in body-image napalm that ignites
on contact with libido. At fourteen
you see it all, then close your eyes and march
into the swamps, jungles, and firefights
that bind you to the television screen
heart first, mind next, whatever war can parch.

EMPATHY

She, a survivor's daughter; you, her friend,
untouched by that or any holocaust
(your father suffered only good looks lost
to stress, to gin, to dinners without end)—
you two unwittingly have joined a trend.
Your "victory over food" pact will exhaust
potassium—cookies counted, later tossed,
deplete your young frames as they try to mend.

No matter that each glossy magazine
flaunts the poor matchstick models of your day,
and mothers bake behind a TV screen
where jungle battles fade into the gray.
Not narcissism (normal in a teen)
but empathy has gotten in your way.

BALLET ROUTINE

Curves on a graph controlled by x and y
express acceleration or decline.
But on your hips, what do they signify:
Each muscle winning, losing your design?

Plié, et dégagé, et balancé,
you're at the *barre* with seven other girls
all beating legs in rhythm as you sway
to strict piano music that unfurls
a private wish to conquer every ounce
of flesh spanning each crested ilium,
each arc held hostage, mute as you all bounce
and stretch your bodies, hurting, healing them.

And then the class is over: time to meet
for pizzas, ice cream cones, across the street.

UNDERSTUDY

If that were you, they'd shout, "Yes! Sing it for us!"
Out in the spotlight—that's where you belong,
not here, buried alive within the chorus,
waiting and hoping something will go wrong.

She is so bright, the star you study under
obliterates your sky. You mustn't show it.
Just sweetly sing while dreaming of your plunder,
and blithely smile in hopes that she won't know it.

Of course she knows; your smile's as fake as hers.
In *Trial By Jury*, she's the jilted bride
and you're a bridesmaid. No pretense endures
Gilbert and Sullivan's rollicking ride.

But since you've not yet learned satiric mettle,
your stomach sours, turns, and cannot settle.

Fifteen Minutes at Juilliard

Auditioning without a repertoire?
Your Mom's connections put you on the spot.
She has you walk in toting your guitar
to show all things are possible—or not.

With good pitch and a sweet but untrained voice
you're used to singing anything you want to,
picking out chords to strum. That was your choice
until, this year, you learned about Bel Canto,

but too late. You perform "If I Had Wings
Like Noah's Dove," "Along the Purple Heather,"
and "I Know Where I'm Going."
                                        Pack your things.
Today you know she's lost it altogether,
wasted your time, strung and unstrung your gut—
velvet-lined case reopened, filled, and shut.

NECKING

If you and your boyfriend sat on the couch
your mom would arrive to break
the silence with a tempting dish
of snacks she'd learned to make
in her new gourmet cooking class.
Was it also a class in how
to keep her nubile daughter
away from sex? Since Roe
was still years off, a cheesy spread
might be one way to turn your head.

Two Conversations

"Just like your mother!" "No, sir, I am fully
aware and rational, and leaving soon.
But you? You have no need to be a bully.
Where is the kind sage I recall from noon?"

And in that moment, you and Dad discover
a rusted iron bond has turned to gold.

What of the specter he invokes? She'll hover
throughout your home and mind, scheming to hold
you back. Is she in fact a witch, a Fury?
Or can you conjure up a magic key
to unlock her mind, too—Socratic query
she'll dodge by redesigning endlessly
your plain clothes, curly hair, unpainted face?

This other dialogue does not take place.

VAMOS

This was one of two words
you and they shared—two college boys
from Guadalajara who spent
a weekend in Puerto Vallarta
like your family from New York

Vamos into the ocean
where you stood as it pulled you
lightly to and fro
until you felt a stronger
wave and laughed together

Vamos to go deeper
but *No* you led them back
to the beach where they inscribed
with angular letters their names
and addresses in your sketchbook

and you never wrote to them

ADOLESCENCE

How can I study?
Why do I frown?
Kicking and screaming you plow through the town.

Who will adore me?
Will it take time?
Kicking and screaming you scribble in rhyme.

Are these my parents?
What do we share?
Kicking and screaming you try not to care,

try to keep singing,
blocking out home,
kicking and screaming from morning till gloam.

Bicycle pedals
bound to a gear,
kicking and screaming you ride through your fear.

Is there a poem
fit for today?
Kicking and screaming you pedal away.

BECOMING BUDDHIST

The summer of learning to type
you also slogged to the river with Siddhartha
and analyzed dreams in the shallows
as Dr. Sigmund dictated the code.

Thinking you knew their source
made dreams seem safe, but Hesse was a puzzle
suffused with Eastern sentiments, ideas
you seldom understood.

So when you awoke at night
with fingers typing "nothing" on the blanket
over and over, you blamed nihilism
or adolescent darkness.

But no: you were absorbing
what to expect in order
to be content.

CREDO-IN-PROGRESS

I. Tough Customer

A stubborn teen, you needed to find out
what life was for, whether it had a point.
"I won't go on, God, till you let me know.
So tell me now or set me free." You waited,
and God did both. "Brilliant!" you said. "You win.
I'll give you a few years—but I'll be watching.
You're going to have to show me every day
that you're still there." You heard, or felt, a rumble
that may have been laughter, as if the deal
were sealed.

II. Anything to Declare?

Presented with the light
at seventeen, you chose
to turn back, stay a while,
having seen that joy
kept an outpost here.
        And what was hovering *there*?
        No prophets, true believers,
        or any kind of shadow.
Because your life is made
of unexpected gifts,
you won't turn one away
without looking to see
what light it holds.

III. An Invocation

*Temperamental universe in whose purpose
(known, unknown, unknowable) we are swimming,
safe within your energy and your chaos:
make me your prism.*

LETTING HER GET AWAY WITH IT

Your mother learned to keep men in their place,
to slap one who's impetuous or rude,
especially if she wasn't in the mood.
Then why not slap a daughter? Leave no trace,
no broken bones, no scarring on your face,
certainly no internal injury.
What better way is there to make you see
she's still the boss and you've fallen from grace?

Today is different. You have had enough
and vow to let her know this slap's her last.
She's not the only one who can play rough.
But your strength scares you, and you draw back fast.

Not for her sake, but yours, your snap decision:
You just don't want to spend your life in prison.

SONG OF FLIGHT

Take all of these: my childhood books, my dolls,
phonograph records from a certain day
I couldn't share with you. Peace of mind calls
and I can only find it far away,
or so it seems. What is this gnawing pain?
It sends me spinning from the grassy hill here
that seemed to be my deepest love's terrain
until a sinkhole yawned in the familiar—

familial pain. What is its form, my form?
What difference does it make how I am seen?
The search for sanity becomes a storm
I must ride out, because I am eighteen.

But you, my little sister, have no hand
in this. I hope someday you'll understand.

DYNAMIC STABILITY

Your classmate asserts that poets
are those who can walk through the aisle
of a moving train without holding
onto straps or poles or shoulders.

You know he intends a metaphor
but you are intent on practicing
and mastering the skill.
Amtrak conductors look harried

or have no sense of humor
when you arrive as a runaway
with a beat-up, broken-locked suitcase
still practicing your balance.

During the ride and the days
that follow, you never stumble,
never look back while soaring.
Numb, you pace yourself,

stay with a friend, accept
the first job you are offered
and maintain a dizzy precision
to quell or diminish your envy

of those whose parents stayed
together, those who walked
through the aisle with adult hands to hold.

FATHER'S GIFTS

I. Sixth Sense

Dad is the one you trust, the one with whom
your golden bond endures across an ocean.
You feel as if he's just in the next room
in case you need to settle some commotion,
as on the evening you turn twenty-one
in Paris. A wild drive, *à grande vitesse,*
ends at a nightclub with a zoo—what fun,
though terror almost makes you pee your dress.

Back at the borrowed flat, you think of him
in New York, where it's five hours behind
and therefore still your birthday. On a whim,
you call. He's just walked out, but strange, his mind
says *No! Go back!* He thinks he's left something
at home, opens the door, hears the phone ring.

II. Voucher

Dad is the one who always said, "You can
do anything you set your mind to do."
Marry a Frenchman?? When your life began,
his country's troops were losing Dien Bien Phu,
some two decades ago. It's no surprise
Papá speaks British English; here's the Strait
daytrippers cross for souvenirs and fries.
Here, too, on TV, Saigon's desperate state.

But you find unknown colors, unknown calm,
begin to dream in French, and then on waking
learn how to peel potatoes in your palm
and slice them into thin sticks without breaking.
Your life can sizzle now. Or, to unlock it,
here's Dad's return-flight voucher in your pocket.

MOTHER'S DAY REMEMBERED

Far from where your fierce glance and hers can meet,
a laundromat on Rue des Pyrenées
is where you learn to fold a fitted sheet—
which, in a different language, seems OK.

The *parisienne* who shows you how to place
your hands in the sheet's corners, shake it straight,
then bring both palms together, is an ace
at teaching without judging. *(Why so late?)*

At 21 you are a cultured waif,
a refugee from family politics
into another mess where you felt safe
with hasty marriage thrown into the mix.

Does this kind-hearted stranger know, or care,
that her instruction holds a hidden prayer?

RAS LE BOL

A phrase you often heard in '74
as a new bride in France was *ras le bol:*
"fed up." With what? Oh, nothing personal,
just *les Etats-Unis*—and with the war
in Vietnam, if you insist.
                       When he
first took you to the beach, you wore a long dress
and promptly soaked the hem in brine. His brother
stage-whispered to him, *Elle n'est pas rentable:*
"She isn't worth it." But why bother trying
to make sense of one arrogant expression

or the other? Because you had to know
what you were up against. And anyhow,
couldn't *ras le bol* also mean brimming,
exploring, overflowing one's own shore,
or simply (as you were) running away?

LETTER SPACE

You've given up living among the French,
abandoned residency paperwork.
Armed with a trade—typography—you clench
your teeth in post–Vietnam War New York.

In setting type, you must pay full attention
to space above, below, between black shapes
flashed onto photo paper. Their dimension
and style affect the meaning that escapes
their boundaries onto a shining field
of white in which you recognize a word.

You savor this. Sharp focus has revealed
you can survive alone, if you're not stirred
too often or too deeply when you find
a letter from the one you left behind.

DESSERTED

The kind whose steady crush whispers between
your teeth as you move closer to its flame
of chocolate, knowing all along you mean
to bask a moment, then repeat the game:
this is but one of many. Some are chilling
and smooth, others can crackle with their heat,
their chips or pools of flavor never filling
your need for something certain, something sweet.

You open, taste, chew and consume them all,
then toss away their packaging resigned
that you, whatever time it takes, will call
them out from where they hide. Thus undermined

your pleasure turns to punishment; your mind
turns to automaton; you turn unkind.

EMERGENCY

The phone rings, and your legs turn to spaghetti.
You try to sprint the few blocks to the train,
then to the hospital. You aren't ready
for grown-up life. Your new husband, in pain,
sedated, hand crushed in a printing press,
lies bandaged, hot and numb. You draw the curtain,
feel sorry for yourself and your distress.
How can his life and yours be so uncertain?

A mania, a waking dream, enfolds you—
technicians, nurses, everyone in sight
trapped in the mozzarella web that holds you
to pizza, marinara, every night.

Your husband's hand recovers. Lost in food,
you fend off thought and cling to attitude.

ROYAL HOTLINE, 1983

*"The Princess is believed to have suffered from bulimia
nervosa, [which] afflicts millions of American women."*
— *"Di's Private Battle," People Magazine*, August 3, 1992

*Soon, Princess Di, you'll lend this thing your name,
crowning a hushed disease with regal grace.
Beauty salons will buzz; women will claim
to know you. But for now I stuff my face
and then go toss my cookies at the throne
in secret. Are we sisters, who have yet
to learn this malady is fashion's clone?
And meanwhile, where's my image? I forget.*

*Maybe I left it by the forced-air dryer,
tucked in a magazine, or by the sink
where a woman's hands massaged my scalp for hire.
Wait, here's a doctor's number. Do you think
he'll help close the two decades, plus or minus,
that I've been kneeling like Your Royal Highness?*

ANALYSIS

I.

Considering the losses—Mother's mind,
part of your own mind, part of every day
spent bingeing, purging all the sweets you find,
embittering yourself—is there a way
that you can ever be a loving mother?
And do you wish to be? It's all a blur.
Time to consult one expert or another.
An analyst will give your thoughts a whir
and let them clear. You talk, you write, you dream:

*It's winter. In my parents' house, I've found
an upstairs bathroom window fogged with steam.
I open, look down at a frozen pond.
There, through the ice, I notice from above
a baby, still alive. This I could love.*

II.

*I run downstairs and out into the cold
to crack the frozen pond and save the child.
With brittle fingers, I can barely hold
my hands in icy water. In a wild
moment I lift her into the night air.
She gasps, and then lets out—a melody.*

You wake and write it down. Soon, on a tear,
you eat and breathe music. You hear, smell, see,
and touch the fibers of harmonic straw,
spinning them into contrapuntal gold,
then diving back for more. All that you draw
from dreams you can deliver hundredfold.

Your mind was never barren, this is true.
But what about a real child? *Yes. That too.*

THE SPILL

Happily pregnant, still you are not free:
a food addict. The child you carry grows
and offers hope that life holds harmony,
yet dissonance remains. Your formless clothes
and disappearing shape maintain some grace
thanks to a necklace your own mother strung
from black, blue, silver beads. That and your face
remind you you're still feminine, still young,
still glowing in a way you can't recall
since childhood, when you loved your mother's voice.
Bending to lose your breakfast in a stall,
you hear beads pouring to the floor. No choice
but crawl to pick them up—this, for the urge
to stuff yourself past hunger and then purge.

WRONG-WAY DRIVER

I. Close Call

Returning home at twilight from the store—
your baby safely strapped into her seat,
the main road not yet widened into four,
then six lanes—in your northbound path you meet
two headlights. Is he crazy? Suicidal?
You swerve onto the shoulder but, for reasons
unknown, you spin around. Your shrill recital
of "No!" explodes the day, the night, the season.

You don't know how you did it, but you land
across the road, turned in the right direction,
stopped on the southbound shoulder. What calm hand
has helped? The baby slumbers in perfection.

Arriving home alarmed, you phone your parents:
You're still alive! The day before, you weren't.

II. Adrenaline Speaks

Here on this shoulder is your place to watch
the wrong-way driver who missed killing you.
Still in his wrong-lane, slow-motion approach,
interior lights all lit, he barrels through
your consciousness again. He can't be real.
He has the spirit of a broken brick
throwing itself against a porcelain wall.
He's grabbed your life and given it a kick.

Was this enough? Is this what was required
to make you value each day as a gift,
or will you linger on, stubbornly mired
in everyday sensation till you drift
downstream leaving no more than alibi?
Here on this shoulder is your place to cry.

SERENDIPITY

A classmate in the writing seminar
you've entered as a back-to-life transition
loves sonnets as you do, but he is far
removed from present-day, lost in tradition.

You tell him that he shows readers no love,
and he agrees: he scarcely loves himself.
He says he may have been the one who drove
toward you, wrong lane, that other night. His health
unravels as he speaks. His nerves are fraying.
He stows his keys and asks you for a ride.
This could have been a game, but no one's playing.
You drive him home, and then yourself, then glide
downstairs and listen to Brahms' Fourth three times.

Your neurons resonate in tonal rhymes.

THE CURE

Could music, poetry, have cured what tugged
your spirit down? Or else, should you believe
doubters who claim you must be shocked or drugged
before an illness will pack up and leave?

They say: *Any disease that's worth its name*
demands a cure that's solid, not imagined.
Therefore the plague you say you overcame
was no more real than the fake cure you've fashioned,
no more substantial than the energy
you say you now have found for doing good.
Such errors come to light whenever we
come to our senses—as you know you should.

Your heart is true. How can your head be wrong?
You have been been cured by friendship, words, and song!

WELL

You're well now, but you're not the one he married,
not anymore. Who was that girl again
who couldn't cross a threshold unless carried?
She'd left her courage where she'd left her pen
some years before he found her. Sweet and damaged,
neurotic and confused, she was just right
for one who saw himself as disadvantaged.
He'd feed her, comfort her, prevent her flight.

Did he inspire you? What sparks did he summon?
His mother even more a wounded soul
than yours, you had a tragedy in common.
Too soon, you shared a life out of control.

Until you clambered out of your own spell,
he knew you. But he never knew you *well*.

THE POSTPONED CONVERSATION

Some days her mind begins to reappear.
Today you feel her halting fingers trace,
along your skull, the curls she used to fear,
although she raised you in a gentler place
than where her classmates called her "kinky head"
or worse. She thinks she's cringing by her locker,
until she sees you there. "Sorry I said
those things," she whispers. Late regrets unblock her.

When you were sixteen, she was being kind,
searing your scalp with chemicals to free
you of the curls she gave you. In her mind
the only truth out there was cruelty.

Here, now, she loves your hair. Grasping your brush
she soothes you, coaxes you. Don't question. Hush.

BULIMIA

On learning you've emerged of late
from that poor sullen porcelain state,
my mind attempts to reenact
your race to be not what you ate—

before your purgatorial bowl
not caring whether you were whole,
existing just to pre-subtract
some pound of flesh that gripped your soul.

Clasping your hand, I wonder why
you spill no tears upon the fact.
Your tears well spent, your starving eye
forsakes the bowl, reclaims the sky.

PART III

What Loves Me Back?

THE GATE REOPENS

My father taught me not to fear
a moment of forgetting.
"If it's important," he said,
"you will remember it."
With Mom and me he watched
on black-and-white TV
families divided by barbed wire
as the Berlin Wall went up.

No sooner did it fall
than he was on a plane.
He would cross Checkpoint Charlie,
walk through the Brandenburg Gate,
bring us back shards of concrete
spray-painted and demolished,
fluorescent green graffiti words
divided, not forgotten.

AD MAN

Dear Dad: You never mentioned that the copy
you gave me of a liquor advertisement
bearing your face was not a magazine ad
as I had thought for years. It was a billboard.

Over what highways I may never know,
but you presided for some weeks or months—
you and your dreamy eyes, good-natured half-smile,
smooth personality in black and white—

poured over drivers. Was it in Chicago,
Detroit, Indianapolis, New Orleans?
Your image claimed "the bourbon man's bourbon"
was chic and yet benign, considering

how wholesome you appeared against the skyline.
My question's not about the role of liquor,
but advertising—that conveyor belt
of want over need, the career that chose you

when journalism didn't seem enough
to fuel the dreams you and my mother had.
You were no model (other than this once)
but an account executive for movie

projectors and cars, in a flashy business
that later spat you out. Where will I find
the box that holds that picture? And why was it
your friend, not you, who told me what it was?

PARTING WORDS
for one suffering from aphasia

She's parting company with her vocab-
ulary and embracing it goodbye.
No need to cut herself on the inev-
itable thorns of words and phrases she
has loved like children, friends, and foreign vis-
itors who lift their luggage now to leave.
And so must she, within her dulling glos-
sary, behind her thinning veil of words.
She isn't well, or ill, but only shriv-
eling back into this one rose whose buds
unfold into the children, verses, vase
she once inhabited.

LANDLOCKED

In time and with regret
water deserts the brain.
You learn how to forget
with grace, to ignore pain,
to let each moment pass.
Here in this landlocked place
time alone flows. The glass
does not contain your face.

HER MEMORY

after electroconvulsive therapy

Mom was a blessing once,
a vibrant tapestry,
until they took away
her woven synergy.

They must not have explained
how changed her mind might be.
They could not have considered
what her young child would see.

Although her inner strength
turned into cruelty,
her earliest bright stitches
dance through my memory.

Clusters of colored threads
trailing out randomly
unfastened from the cloth
tell me her soul is free.

Today or any day
each childhood reverie
becomes another blessing
that weaves itself to me.

MARATHON

We never think she'll go until she's gone.
The painful circumstances hardly matter,
considering it's been a marathon

and not a sprint. Her spirit will have won.
We may have noticed her attention scatter
but never thought she'd let go. If she's gone

she cannot give us her opinions on
the world of art, but we'll recall her patter
and know her life has been a marathon.

With chaos turned to grace, she is a swan.
No longer do her helpers have to clatter
machines so she won't leave us. Is she gone?

Her blessing stays, distributed upon
our heads and hearts, where we have always had her.
Our lives already were her marathon.

Her final words to me, just after dawn,
were about airline ticket prices—chatter
I never thought I'd hear. Then she was gone.
Now we perpetuate the marathon.

On Your Birthday, In Your Absence

I light a candle in a frog-shaped holder—
a smiling clay gargoyle. You would approve,
although you'd try not to. As I grew older
you feared my brand of whimsy would remove
all hope that I could grow to be a lady.
What did that mean to you? A son-in-law
who might still be around when you were eighty?
You didn't make it either. It's a draw.
Smoke rises, red wax melts. Who'd tell our story
if none of us had learned to float above
our humorless abyss, or learned that worry
was only an expression of your love?
Wax trickling down his sides, the frog keeps grinning.
Your laughter seals the end to the beginning.

BARRIER REEF

> *"Some of the [New York] subway cars... are deep*
> *underwater now."*
> —Jen Carlson, *The Gothamist,* Oct. 23, 2015.

Before this was an underwater room
it clattered over borough boundaries
toward the museum. Inside, Mother taught me

to look at human faces and imagine
painting or drawing them. But I changed trains:
poetry, music, anything but pictures.

The subway rumbled on, malodorous
and dingy till, steam-cleaned and streamlined, this car
was dumped into Atlantic coastal waters.

There is no clatter now unless a boat
of scuba divers visits to record
silver or pink striped fins propelling you

through and around these unbarred doors and windows.
Seaweed enrobes passenger seats, poles, walls,
strap-hanger straps, floors, ceilings. Welcome, fish,

to urban decay. As you ride the current
darting about for food or spawning grounds,
your images flow through my eyes and mingle

with memories in a now-open mind.
There is no barrier left to stop your likeness
from swimming onto watercolor paper.

PAINTBOX

Arranged in a spectral ladder,
flanked by a sable brush,
eight color tablets on a blending platter
invite me in to wash

the tedium from a plain day,
infuse it with a hue.
I lift the mixture up and let it play
where paper leads it through

a hall of crooked mirrors,
a capillary chute
to rinse an image free of any errors
adhering to its root.

You bloom out of the pallor.
My brush comes to a rest.
The page now filled with unimagined color,
I am its grateful guest.

An Unfinished Portrait

Play with me, she calls from the glossed wood easel
cornered on a porch over sunlit flagstone—
calls to me, who's hurrying past with coffee.
Soon there's a smashed cup,

punctured foot. Cross-purposes have arrived to
bleed me now. Why did I begin a portrait?
So much else was waiting to be completed.
Why even bother

looking back, remembering who I might be
other than accounts and statistics well kept,
better kept than colorful pencils, charcoals,
cloth and erasers

tempting me with shadows and lights to borrow
minutes, hours, days from a world that can't care?
Stay with me, she calls as I hobble out for
soap, water, clean gauze,

since the world won't barter for one more minute
reconciling spirit with mind and matter.
Washing, dabbing, pressing the wound, I hear her
still in the distance—

Yes, you must. I guess she won't stop cajoling,
she who gleams, demands and deserves attention,
one more shard of beauty among the wreckage:
Never ignore me.

SKATING LESSON

I.

The music starts. I glide, I seek nothing,
await nothing, lean into curves, discover
how a turn signal becomes the turn itself.
Raised hands spin me, turn me into a pilot
who will sacrifice control for a touch
gained by spurning gold, a winning streak
born of ambition's absence.

II.

Over the ice
no assertion,
only surrender.

Not to be courted,
rolled or cajoled,
the current I ride

never foreseen,
only awaited,
learned without asking.

III.

Compressed below the ice, embossed in lines
smaller than circles scratched in its face,
hidden in corners the Zamboni misses,
dreams are the turns I close my eyes to skate.

IV.

Under the frozen surface of a pond
was a baby. I ran to break the crust,
and found the child alive.

From this dream I gathered,
Yes, have children.

The message had a hibernating twin:
Ice will revive you.

V.

What is this new force, then, that pushes outward
from a dream's center, gliding, stroking, spinning?
Ice has become a friend that teaches silence
because it has no way of saying *never,*
impossible, regret, or even *beauty.*

TWO ARCS

*"Johnny Boychuk injury: Bruin stretchered off ice after
hit into boards"* —Sporting News, 12/5/13

The online video reruns his crash
every four seconds from three different angles.
Checked hard into the boards, the hockey player
crumples, jumps back, then once more races toward them.
I drag my eyes away,

read how his teammates helped him with the stretcher,
how he was conscious, moving his limbs, speaking,
as I was years ago when I fell backward
skating some unambitious figures, testing
new blades poorly attached.

Not bad to rest an injured head on ice—
but staring up at lights, how could I tell
if I'd blacked out? There was no instant replay,
no steep dive into Lethe but a short dip,
floating, surfacing

into the glare as EMS arrived
to brace my neck and check me. No concussion,
it might as well have been a coffee nap:
You take a long, deep sip of java, close
your eyes till they spring open.

Living—the opposite—jars you awake
and catapults you into an awareness
that tilts toward the end
abruptly or not
into a different sleep.

PORTRAIT AT DUSK

This is the "after" picture you see now—
after a clutch of losses, false beginnings,
unruly endings. Those cling to her brow
and to each set of corners, while the winnings
swim in her eyes and balance on her lips
to tilt and roll according to each morning's
peculiar cast of light, solar eclipse,
sweet-sour recollections, bitter warnings.
And what was here before? Unfounded hope,
parental expectations and her own:
expecting glibly to be loved, to cope
with everything and never be alone.
The sun's embers, the evening's giddy breeze—
they've startled her. Another moment, please.

IN THE CELLAR

Some stories are not told
but stored in airtight vessels
with time and other solvents.

On odd days I descend,
adjust the failing lamp,
and agitate the specimens.

Each sealed in a dim pool,
they swirl on dusky currents,
feed on the dark, and ripen.

One day they appear translucent.
How quickly I've outlived them!
Will I someday grow old

enough to speak of them?
Meanwhile I dust the glass
and again revise the labels.

THE FAMILY BOOKLET

We'd paid a visit to the consulate,
pronounced our vows inside a backyard tent,
and then received a dainty document
designed as future-birth certificate—
a *Livret de Famille* from your French state
with greetings, iced in glossy white and meant
to stimulate the thoughts of those intent
on following its message: Procreate.

I fan the tissue-paper leaves that wait,
decades later, for names of our first ten
enfants. Our fragile bond would desiccate
too soon, but empty pages mock again
this would-be family sealed forevermore
and baked into a wedding *petit four*.

SOUP IN LYON

A carrot, an onion, two eggs,
a baguette with a pat of butter,
maybe coffee or tea, maybe milk:
for one season these carried the day

in a city where silk had been golden,
where a tooth-puller's puppet, Guignol,
beat policemen and scoffed at the landlord;
where the chef was philosopher-priest.

A small bicycle folded, unfolded,
bore me up and around on the ancient
Croix-Rousse hill that I see some nights
in dreams of a city whose *haute*

cuisine I had missed but did not miss
as I learned to be pleased by basics:
morning market, a pot on the stove
with two eggs, a large carrot, an onion,

half for now and the rest for later;
a baguette with a half-pat of butter,
maybe coffee or tea, maybe milk,
and maybe an apple with cheese.

Any more? Any more would be excess
for I fed my eyes and ears
on the shapes of streets and rivers,
and my mouth on the shapes of words.

WHAT LOVES ME BACK?

Broccoli Ex Post Facto
Her trick, to make me savor it,
was saying "Look, your favorite!"
And soon it was,
with butter sauce,
even without.
There is no doubt
I owe my health
to Grandma's stealth.

Yogurt Unmasked
The kind with sugared fruit jam at its base,
or even coffee syrup, had a place
at home and school. It took me years to see
that yogurt—*plain*—might feed longevity.
For granting bones and stomach such a favor,
I've learned to love its tart, peculiar flavor.

Brown Rice, Browned
When rinsed before boiling, each grain is a pearl.
Submerged—two parts water—they gather to swirl
and circle the bubbling channels of steam,
then toast for a moment. To taste is to dream.

cont'd

Onion Affair
I slice you to get rings. You make me weep.
Oiling a pan, I dump you there and stir
until you sizzle in a fragrant heap,
sweeter and more transparent than you were.

Ode to an Everything Bagel
Delicious inclusivity, whose mound
of hummus, or cream cheese with Nova Scotia,
complements seeds, grains, onion strips well browned—
I don't care whether you're *halal* or *kosher*.

Graffiti for Grapefruit
You are the key to morning,
my sweet and not-so-sweet.
One kiss with little warning
rallies me from defeat,
from days stumbling back-assward.
Your tart taste is the password.

COMFORT FOOD

Lentils and barley,
water and salt,
split peas and pasta—
pure to a fault—

stir until clouded,
season to taste,
boil and then simmer,
nothing to waste.

Greens can be added.
Time's on a loop.
Towers have toppled
into the soup.

Cauldron of comfort
served with warm hands,
this is a recipe
crisis demands.

ACKNOWLEDGMENTS

The author would like to thank editors of the following publications, where some of these poems first appeared, sometimes in an earlier version:

Aethlon (Skating Lesson, Two Arcs)
American Arts Quarterly (Portrait at Dusk)
Amsterdam Quarterly (Guidance, Hide and Seek)
Beltway Poetry (Vamos, Ras le Bol, The Gate Reopens)
The Brazen Head (Becoming Buddhist, Credo-in-Progress)
Expansive Poetry Online (Beach Mosaic, Shading, Fingerpaint, Childhood Revised, Grace, An Awakening, First Valentine, Detailing a Picture Frame, Home Economics, Necking, Letting Her Get Away With It, Dynamic Stability, Serendipity [as "Empathy II"], Her Memory, Marathon, Barrier Reef, An Unfinished Portrait, What Loves Me Back [as "Epicurigrams"])
First Things (Mother's Day Remembered, The Postponed Conversation, Comfort Food)
Life & Legends (Analysis)
Loch Raven Review (Soup in Lyon)
Lucid Rhythms (On Your Birthday, in Your Absence)
Mezzo Cammin (Mountain Fire, Understudy, Fifteen Minutes at Juilliard, Song of Flight, Father's Gifts, Letter Space)
New Verse Review (Morning, 1956)
The Orchards (Well)
Pen in Hand (Discovering Classical Music, Ad Man)
Per Contra (The Dining Room War 1967, Desserted)
Pulsebeat (Under the Piano)
The Road Not Taken (On Reading the Encyclopedia, Emergency)
The Rotary Dial (Atlantic Beach, Aunt Rose, Antiseptic, The Woman Who Jumped, Mozart's Alphabet, Announcement, Ballet Routine, Two Conversations, Royal Hotline, Wrong-Way Driver, The Cure, Paintbox, The Family Booklet)
Shit Creek Review (In the Cellar)
Snakeskin (Dollhouse, Adolescence)
Sow's Ear Poetry Journal (Home Movie, circa 1960)
String Poet (Perfect Time, Getting Lost, Parting Words)
Trinacria (Empathy, Bulimia, Landlocked)
Verse-Virtual (Handedness, Somewhere in the San Fernando Valley)

ADDITIONAL ACKNOWLEDGMENTS

Gratitude to dear poets and friends—including Indran Amirtha-
nayagam, Melissa Balmain, Al Basile, Sandra Beasley, Laura J.
Bobrow, Tom Cable, Grace Cavalieri,
Maryann Corbett, Rod Deacey, Rhina Espaillat, Fred Feirstein,
Conrad Geller, Dana Gioia, Sam Gwynn, Ruth Holzer, Betsey
Houghton, Mark Jarman, Allison Joseph, Mike Juster, Julie
Kane, Mary Kipps, Phillis Levin, Shirley Lim, Stephen Marcus,
Susan McLean, Joshua Mehigan, Richard Moore, Art Morten-
sen, Rick Mullin, Alfred Nicol, George Owens, Aaron
Poochigian, Val Rush, Jan Schreiber, Alicia Stallings, Timothy
Steele, Fred Turner, Deborah Warren, Leanne Wiberg, and oth-
ers I'll inevitably think of
tomorrow—who offered valued knowledge and feedback on my
poems, whether in a class, critique group, tutorial, or
conversation. Gratitude to Elaine Babitz, Suzanne Mazel, Shari
Narva, and Linda Tartell, for helping to confirm various memo-
ries and explain a few things. Many thanks to Alan Abrams for
his inspired work on this book and for believing in it. And spe-
cial thanks to Molly Peacock for helping me see that I must
write this book, and showing me how to start.

ABOUT THE AUTHOR: Claudia Gary is a poet, composer, instructor, editor, visual artist, and health/science journalist who lives in the Washington, DC area. She teaches workshops on sonnets, villanelles, meter, persona poems, "Poetry vs. Trauma," and more, at The Writer's Center (writer.org) and privately, via videoconference. Her first full-length collection was *Humor Me* (David Robert Books, 2006). Her chapbooks include *Ripples in the Fabric, Schadenfreud(e), Bikini Buyer's Remorse, Let's Get Out of Here, The Grateful Guest, Epicurigrams, Genetic Revisionism,* and *Someone Likes You.* Her poems appear in anthologies and journals internationally.

Claudia's musical works include tonal chamber music and song settings of poems by Frederick Turner, Dana Gioia, Phillis Levin, Frederick Feirstein, Micheal O'Siadhail, Kelly Cherry, Indran Amirthanayagam, and Rhina Espaillat, as well as Shakespeare, Marvell, and Heine. Her setting for soprano, violin, and cello of Shakespeare's sonnet XVIII ("Shall I compare thee to a summer's day?") appeared in issue 60 (1992) of *Sparrow, the Yearbook of the Sonnet.*

A semifinalist for the Anthony Hecht Prize (Waywiser), Pushcart Prize nominee, and three-time finalist in the Howard Nemerov Sonnet Contest, Claudia is a former poetry editor (*Edge City Review*), former publisher (*Musings from Northern Virginia*), and a current editorial advisory board member of *New Verse Review.* A former impresario (The Leesburg Poetry & Chamber Music Series; The Poetry Exchange with Richard Moore), she has presented panels and guest talks at the West Chester University (Pa.) Poetry Conference, Frost Farm Poetry Conference, ALSCW, Poetry by the Sea, Eastern Shore Writers Association, and DC Science Writers Association.

Claudia created and taught "The Poetry of Science & the Science of Poetry" for FAES.org at NIH in 2019, and now teaches an equivalent course at The Writer's Center, via videoconference. Claudia's essay about setting poems to music is at https://straightlabyrinth.info/conference.html. See also https://www.pw.org/directory/writers/claudia_gary.

The author reads at Carmine Street Metrics
(at Otto's Shrunken Head), NYC.
Photo by Rick Mullin

www.ingramcontent.com/pod-product-compliance
Lightning Source LLC
Chambersburg PA
CBHW040125150726
48005CB00015B/2376